Here Comes Diwali
the festival of lights

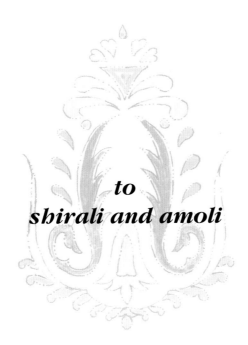

**to
shirali and amoli**

by **meenal pandya**

recipes by *Laxmi Jain*

Second Edition

with easy recipes and fun activities for children

Published by:

MeeRa Publications
P.O.Box 812129
Wellesley, MA 02482 - 0014
781 . 235 . 7441

www . MeeRaPublications . com

Illustrations by: Ashish Mehta
Book Design by: Signature DESIGN
                    SDesignrs@aol.com

ISBN : 0-9635539-3-3

Printed in Hong Kong

Just as a single

Lamp can bring

Light in a moonless night

Hope in the darkest hour

Inspiration to even the faintest of heart

May this Diwali

Bring you

A new light

A new hope

A new inspiration

To make a difference

In your life

In your family

In your neighborhood

In your world

Happy Diwali

"Diwali is coming," Mom says.

Everyone is getting ready.

"Diwali is the festival of lights," Grandma explains.

Mom and Dad are cleaning the whole house,
washing windows, painting walls, cleaning every corner,
and polishing every piece of furniture.

The house looks sparkling clean.

The kitchen smells so..o..o. good.
Mom is making lots of sweets and snacks.

My favorite sweet is besan laddoo.

"Mom, may I have some please?"

"No, we must first offer them to Goddess Laxmi, so
she can bless our food before we eat,"
says Mom.

"It is rangoli time" says my sister.
She brings her favorite colored powder.

We sit on the floor and paint colorful
flowers and patterns.

Mom is making hundreds of wicks today
for all the oil lamps.

I help mom put the lamps on windowsills,
doorways, and in the garden.

They glow and glimmer in the darkness.

Today, Dad brought firecrackers.

There are rockets that shoot up high in the sky, ground
swirlers that splash sparks as they swirl,
and ones that make really loud noises when they explode.

My whole neighborhood is going to be filled
with the sounds of those firecrackers.

Dhum !! Crack, Zeeeee !!....Dhum, Bhoom !!

Mom says I have to be very careful.
I should not light them without a grown-up watching me.

Diwali is a five day festival and the first day of
Diwali is called Dhanuteras.

"Goddess Laxmi visits every house wearing a
beautiful red sari.
She arrives on an elephant and visits those houses
that are clean and welcoming. She brings wealth, health,
and prosperity, " Grandma explains.

Soon after taking a bath, each one of us shall wear nice,
clean clothes and offer prayers to Goddess Laxmi.

The second day of Diwali is called Narak Chaturdarshi.
In some parts of India, it is also called Kaali-chaudash.

Grandma says that many years ago, Lord Krishna killed a demon named Narakasur and freed sixteen thousand princesses that Narakasur had kidnapped.

So, every year on Narak-chaturdarshi day, people re-member this
victory and celebrate.

Grandma gave me a sweet smelling sandalwood oil to use after my bath.

Tonight we are going to light the lamps
and more firecrackers.

Thousands of years ago Lord Rama, the good and kind hearted prince of Ayodhya, had fought a big battle with the evil King Ravana of Sri Lanka.
Ravana had kidnapped Rama's beloved wife, Sita.
With an entire army of monkeys and bears,
Lord Rama fought this evil king and his army for nine days. Finally he
killed King Ravana and freed Sita.

On Diwali day, which is the third day, the victorious Lord Rama returned to his kingdom of Ayodhya with his wife Sita, and became one of the most beloved kings ever.

The day of Diwali is also the last day of the Hindu year, called Vikram Samvat.

Next day, on New Year's Day, we all wake up very early
in the morning and put on nice new clothes
to go to the temple.

We greet all our friends and family by saying,
"Happy Diwali" and "Happy New Year".

Mom tells me that I should first bow to the elders to
get their blessings. Then I can go and play with my cousins.

Once, many many years ago, on a New Year's Day, Indra,
the God of Rain, became angry with the people on earth,
so he sent
torrential rains flooding every town and village.

Lord Krishna - although a small boy at the time - came to
the rescue. To everyone's amazement, he picked up
Mount Govardhan with one finger and used it as a
gigantic umbrella.

The people stood under the Mountain and were thus
saved by Lord Krishna.

The fifth and last day of Diwali is called Bhaiya Duj.
It is also called Yama- dwitiya.
It is a special day for brothers and sisters.

On this day, sisters invite their brothers over for
dinner.
Brothers bring lovely gifts for their sisters.
They show their love for each other and wish each other
happiness.

My mom invited my uncle and his family over for dinner.
My uncle brought a nice red sari for mom and besan
laddoo for me. I played with my cousins all day.

Diwali is so much fun.
Good food, fun things to do, and so many stories.

I cannot wait for the next Diwali!

Fun Activities

Making Rangoli

Divide a bag of rice in four parts. Add and mix a few drops of different food colors to each part making red, blue, green, and yellow rice.

Take a square wooden board.
(Make sure edges of the borad are not sharp).
Have each child make his or her own design with colored chalk or crayons.

Brush a light stroke of liquid glue filling the design. Now add colored rice in different parts of design - this is essentially similar to coloring.

Note: Traditionally these designs are done with colored rice powder. However, rice grains are easier to work with for children.

Making a Wick

During Diwali time people make several wicks that can be used to light the oil lamps. Small children enjoy making wicks since it allows them to play with cotton balls, and they are delighted when the lamps light up using the wick that they made. There are two kinds of wicks that they can make.

Long Pipe-Like Wick

Take a small piece of cotton from the cottonball. Using both palms roll out a long string-like cotton that is little fat at the middle and sharp at both the ends. A child can make several wicks in a small amount of time.

Stand-up Wick

Grab a little larger part of cotton and create a ball-like base that extends into a tiny sharp end. The base acts as a reservoir for oil and the end takes the oil up for lighting.

At the end of this project, the teacher can light some of these lamps by putting wicks into a small container with little oil.

Making a Clay-Lamp Holder (divi)

Using clay have each child make a
small container or a bowl by using his or her
hand as a base.

If possible have someone with a kiln fire the bowls
that they can decorate or paint later on.

For a longer activity, you can combine the lamp making
and wick making together so that a lanp can be lighted at
the end of the activity.

Easy

Recipes

These recepies are safe for children, since
they do not require the use of a stove.

Besan Laddoo (Sweet Chick-Pea Flour Balls)

2 Cups Chick-Pea flour
3/4 cup sweet butter
1 1/4 cup sugar (according to taste)
1/2 tsp cardamom powder
2 tbsp chopped almonds

In a 2 quart glass bowl, melt butter in a microwave on high heat for about 1 to 2 minutes or until it melts.

Combine chick-pea flour in the melted butter and mix properly.

Microwave the mixture for about 4 minutes at high heat. Remove and stir for about 20 seconds.

Microwave the mixture for 3 minutes at high heat. Stir. Microwave for 2 minutes, remove, and stir it. Microwave again for 3 minutes.

Remove and let it cool for about 40 minutes or until it is cool to touch. Combine sugar, cardamom and chopped almonds. Add it to the mixture.

Take 1/4 cup mixture in palm, press with both hands and roll into small, tight balls.

Store the Laddoo's in an airtight container.
Serves up to 10
Time: 30 minutes.

Special notes;
1.   Timing specified for above recipe is pertinent to 900 W microwave oven. The timing should be adjusted to the microwave oven in use.

2.   The cookware selected should be suitable for microwave use.

Rice Pudding

Rice pudding can be elegantly decorated with chopped almonds, pistachios, and ground cardamom.

6 cups milk
1/4 cup rice
1/2 cup sugar (you may adjust the amount according to your taste)
1.4 tsp cardamom
pinch of saffron

1. Wash the rice throughly. In a 4 quart glass bowl, mix 6 cups of milk and rice and microwave about 20 to 22 minutes.

2. Stir, and remove all the rice lumps in the milk. Microwave for 10 minutes. Stir again and microwave for 10 more minutes.

3. Dissolve the saffron in one-tablespoon water or milk. Mix it into the rice pudding. Add sugar and mix well. Microwave for 10 minutes on high heat.

4. Decorate with chopped almonds and pistachios. Serve warm or chilled.

Serves: 8
Time: 50 minutes

Special notes:
1.　　Timing specified for above recipe is pertinent to 900 W microwave oven. The timing should be adjusted to the microwave oven in use.

2.　　The cookware selected should be suitable for microwave use.

Fruit Cream

2 cups whipped cream
1 cup green grapes
1 cup red grapes
1 cup chopped banana
2 cups strawberry slices
1 tsp vanilla

In a big bowl mix whipping cream, banana, grapes and vanilla.

Decorate with slices of strawberry around the bowl.

Cool in refrigerator for 1 hour before serving.

serves: 8
Time: 20 minutes

Shrikhand

4 cups sour cream
1/2 cup sugar
1/4 tsp cardamom powder
1/4 tsp saffron
1 tbsp milk
1 tbsp chopped almonds and pistachios

Dissolve the saffron in milk. In a 2 quart bowl mix 4 cups of sour cream, sugar and saffron with a mixer or heavy spoon.

Decorate with pistachios, almonds, and cardamom. Cool it in refrigerator for 2 hours before serving.

serves: 8

Time :15 minutes

Glossary

Ayodhya - Name of a city in India where Lord Rama was born

Besan laddoo –traditional sweet balls made out of chickpea flour

Bhaiya Duj - a special day for brothers and sisters

Dhanuteras – part of diwali celebration when goddess of wealth is prayed

Diwali - row of lights, name of a most celebrated Hindu festival

Govardhan -a mountain in the western part of India, named after Lord Krishna

Kaali-chaudash - fourteenth day of lunar calendar and a part of Diwali celebration

Laxmi - Goddess of wealth

Lord Indra - God of Rain

Lord Krishna - Reincarnation of Lord Vishnu

Lord Rama - Reincarnation of Lord Vishnu

Narakasur - a strong demon

Narakchaturdarshi - fourteenth day of lunar calendar and a part of Diwali celebration

Pooja - offering prayers

Rangoli - floor design made out of colored powder or rice

Vikram Samvat - Hindu Year named after the King Vikram

Yama-dwitiya - second day of Vikram Samvat when brothers and sisters celebrate

Word Search

Find the following words in the puzzle below

DIWALI

FESTIVAL

RANGOLI

GOVARDHAN

KRISHNA

RAVANA

LAXMI

LADDOO

WICKS

WEALTH

RAMA

SITA

M	O	N	T	D	I	W	A	L	I	L	X
V	W	P	S	F	Z	E	O	M	A	A	Y
R	Q	I	G	B	M	A	L	V	S	X	I
A	S	D	C	E	R	L	I	G	H	M	I
N	Q	T	N	K	M	T	U	P	H	I	J
G	J	K	R	I	S	H	N	A	Y	O	W
O	A	Z	S	E	I	T	N	V	O	B	R
L	T	R	F	J	T	B	N	D	M	K	A
I	K	L	M	U	A	O	D	R	Y	W	V
R	F	T	G	I	K	A	P	A	Q	G	A
E	B	N	H	M	L	L	N	M	S	B	N
C	G	O	V	A	R	D	H	A	N	T	A

Our goal is to make the vast and beautiful culture of India available to our future generations. We believe that our rich heritage is so vast and yet so complex that unless the proper tools are given, it can get lost either in superficial behavior or rituals. Through our books we strive to bring the subtle beauty and inherent strength of this culture to the practical level where it can live and breathe every day through practice with understanding. To that end, please let us know how we are doing. Your comments and suggestions are always welcome.

Other books by
MeeRa Publications

Pick a Pretty Indian Name for Your Baby

Over six thousand names with their authentic meanings and tips on selecting names that work well in the Western culture.

Price: US $19.95
Number of Pages: 260
ISBN: 0-9635539-0-9

Vivah - Design a Perfect Hindu Wedding

Especially written for brides and grooms who are planning to put together a Hindu wedding. From understanding the significance of the ceremony to finding the hall for the wedding, Vivah will assist you every step of the way. With tips and suggestions throughout the book, you will find yourself not only learning the ropes but also having fun as you go.

Price: US $24.95
Number of Pages: 112
ISBN: 0-9635539-2-5